W9-CIN-006

Edgewood Public Montessori LLC
Okemos, MI

Masterpieces: Artists and Their Works

Mary Cassatt

by Blake A. Hoena

Consultant:
Joan Lingen, Ph.D.
Professor of Art History
Clarke College
Dubuque, Iowa

Bridgestone Books
an imprint of Capstone Press
Mankato, Minnesota

Bridgestone Books are published by Capstone Press
151 Good Counsel Drive, P.O. Box 669, Mankato, Minnesota 56002
http://www.capstonepress.com

Copyright © 2004 Capstone Press. All rights reserved.
No part of this publication may be reproduced in whole or in part, or stored in a retrieval system, or transmitted in any form or by any means, electronic, mechanical, photocopying, recording, or otherwise, without written permission of the publisher.
For information regarding permission, write to Capstone Press,
151 Good Counsel Drive, P.O. Box 669, Dept. R, Mankato, Minnesota 56002.
Printed in the United States of America

Library of Congress Cataloging-in-Publication Data
Hoena, Blake A.
    Mary Cassatt / by Blake A. Hoena.
    p. cm.—(Masterpieces: artists and their works)
    Summary: Discusses the life, works, and lasting influence of Mary Cassatt.
    Includes bibliographical references and index.
    ISBN 0-7368-3408-7 (softcover) ISBN 0-7368-2229-1 (hardcover)
    1. Cassatt, Mary, 1844–1926—Juvenile literature. 2. Artists—United States—Biography—Juvenile literature. [1. Cassatt, Mary, 1844—1926. 2. Artists. 3. Painting, American. 4. Women—Biography.] I. Title. II. Series.
N6537.C35 H64 2004
759.13—dc21
                                                           2003000064

Editorial Credits
Heather Kindseth, series designer; Juliette Peters, book designer; Alta Schaffer, photo researcher; Karen Risch, product planning editor

Photo Credits
Archives of American Art, Smithsonian Institution/Mary Cassatt, after 1900. Research material on Mary Cassatt and James A. MacNeill Whistler 1872–1975, cover (right)
Bridgeman Art Library/Los Angeles County Museum of Art, 4; Mellon Coll., National Gallery of Art, Washington, D.C., USA, 12
Chester Dale Collection, Image 2002 Board of Trustees, National Gallery of Art, Washington, D.C., 20
Chicago Historical Society, 18
Corbis/Philadelphia Museum of Art, 6, 16
Montclair Art Museum, Montclair, N.J., Gift of the Max Kade Foundation, 1958.1, 8
SuperStock/The Huntington Library, Art Collections, and Botanical Gardens, San Marino, CA, cover (left)
The Roland P. Murdock Collection, Wichita Art Museum, Wichita, Kansas, 14
Sterling and Francine Clark Art Institute, Williamstown, Massachusetts, 10

1 2 3 4 5 6 08 07 06 05 04 03

Table of Contents

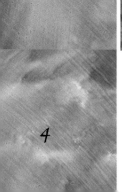

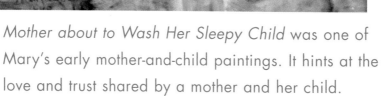

Mother about to Wash Her Sleepy Child was one of Mary's early mother-and-child paintings. It hints at the love and trust shared by a mother and her child.

Mary Cassatt

Mary Cassatt (1844–1926) lived during a time when women were not encouraged to be artists. Most people felt women should stay home and raise a family. They did not think women could support themselves as artists.

Also, Mary was an American. In the 1800s, art critics did not respect American artists. Critics thought Americans knew little about culture and art.

Mary did not let people's ideas about women and Americans stop her. She studied art and worked hard. She became the only American asked to join a group of artists called Impressionists. Mary's talent and hard work earned respect for women and American artists.

Mary created many well-known pieces of art. She is best known for her paintings of family scenes. She especially enjoyed painting mothers with their children, like in *Breakfast in Bed* (shown on cover).

In *Alexander and His Son*, Mary's brother Alexander sits with his son Robert. Mary shows the closeness between father and son by giving them similar serious looks.

Young Mary

Mary was born May 22, 1844, in Allegheny City. This town is now a part of Pittsburgh, Pennsylvania. Her parents were Robert and Katherine Cassatt. Mary had three brothers and one sister.

When Mary was 7, her family moved to Europe. Her parents wanted to show their children European culture. The children learned foreign languages and visited art museums. Mary developed a love for art while in Europe. The Cassatts moved back to the United States in 1855.

At age 16, Mary took classes at the Pennsylvania Academy of Fine Arts. She studied drawing and painting. She also learned about anatomy, the study of the human body. Artists study the human body to learn how to make lifelike pictures and statues of people.

When Mary was 21, she moved to Paris, France. She wanted to study art there. Many famous artists lived in Paris at the time. Paris also had better art schools and museums than the United States did.

The Salon's judges originally rejected *The Young Bride*.
They chose to display it after Mary darkened its background.

Paris

At first, Mary had a hard time in Paris. The main art school, École des Beaux-Arts, did not accept women as students. Teachers at many art schools did not want to teach women.

Mary found other ways to study. She took private painting lessons from art teachers. She also spent a great deal of time at the Louvre Museum in Paris. There, she copied well-known paintings. Artists learn how to paint by copying the work of famous artists.

In 1868, Mary's hard work was rewarded. The Salon displayed her painting *The Mandolin Player*. The Salon was a popular art gallery in Paris. People from around the world came to see the art at the Salon. Artists showing work there often sold their art and gained fame.

Years later, Mary displayed *Ida* and *The Young Bride* at the Salon. These paintings helped her gain respect as an artist. People began to buy her paintings.

In *The Young Woman Offering the Panal to the Toreador*, the people look as if they could be talking. Mary tried to show the relationships between people in her art.

Mary's Travels

During the early 1870s, Mary traveled. She went to Pittsburgh and Chicago to try to sell her work. The Great Fire of 1871 broke out while Mary was in Chicago. The fire destroyed a large part of downtown Chicago. Many of Mary's early paintings were burned in the fire.

In late 1871, Mary traveled to Europe to study. She copied old paintings in Italy. She looked at famous works of art in the Netherlands, Belgium, and Spain.

In Spain, Mary spent several months in the town of Seville. There, she studied Spanish art and painted the people she saw.

While in Seville, Mary's work began to change. Many of her earlier paintings were portraits that used dark colors. Her Seville paintings were more colorful. They showed the colorful costumes of the Spanish people. Mary also began to paint scenes from everyday life while in Seville. These paintings showed people talking with each other.

Little Girl in a Blue Armchair was Mary's first attempt at Impressionism. This painting captures a moment of everyday life by showing a girl sitting in a natural, relaxed way.

Edgar Degas

Mary grew tired of painting in the style that the Salon's judges liked. They wanted to display traditional paintings. These paintings often had dark backgrounds and were very lifelike.

In 1877, Mary met Edgar Degas. Degas belonged to the Impressionists. Members of this art movement included Claude Monet and Auguste Renoir.

Impressionists worked with bright colors and did not worry about painting lifelike pictures. They tried to show how a scene looked at a quick glance. Impressionists used broken brush strokes of one solid color. They did not blend colors together as they painted. This style made their work look splotchy up close. But from a distance, the picture in a painting could easily be seen.

Degas invited Mary to join the Impressionists. In 1879, she displayed 11 paintings at an Impressionist art exhibit in Paris.

The child in *Emmie and her Child* holds his mother's chin with one hand and rests his head on her shoulder. These actions hint at the closeness between mother and child.

Mothers and Children

Mary's paintings are different than other Impressionists. Most Impressionists painted outdoor scenes. Mary liked to paint indoor scenes of people. She wanted to show the relationships between people in her art. Many of her paintings are portraits of her family and friends.

Mary painted people doing everyday activities. She painted people drinking tea, reading the newspaper, going to the theatre, and sewing. Her paintings made everyday events seem important.

One of Mary's favorite subjects was mothers with their children. Mary never married or had children of her own. But in her art, she was able to show the love that mothers and children share.

Mary's art helped show the importance of women in society. By painting women reading, she hinted at their intelligence. By painting mothers, she showed that women are important as caregivers.

In Mary's print *The Letter,* the woman is deep in thought. Mary liked to show women performing everyday activities, such as thinking about a letter.

16

Prints

In 1879, Mary began to create etchings. Etchings are pictures created on a metal plate. Artists cover the plate with ink to make prints of the picture. Etchings allow artists to make many copies of the same picture.

Prints are less expensive to make than paintings. Prints also are cheaper for people to buy. Many artists create etchings so more people can enjoy their work.

Mary joined the Society of Painters-Engravers in the late 1880s. This group of artists made prints. In 1889 and 1890, Mary showed her prints at the Painter-Engravers exhibits in Paris. But in 1891, she was not allowed to display her work with the group. Mary was left out because she was not French.

Mary decided to have her own exhibit. She displayed 10 prints and some of her paintings at an art gallery in Paris. Many of her prints showed women doing simple things, like bathing or dressing. People were amazed by how colorful Mary's prints were.

In the center of *Modern Woman*, a woman handed an apple to a young girl. Mary wanted this scene to show that the hard work of modern women made it easier for young girls to gain knowledge.

Modern Woman

Mary was asked to paint a mural for the 1893 World's Columbian Exposition. This fair in Chicago celebrated advances in manufacturing, science, and art.

Mary's painting was shown in the Woman's Building. This building held displays about important women activists and scientists. It also presented examples of women's arts and crafts from around the world.

Mary called her painting *Modern Woman*. Its center section showed women gathering fruit from the Tree of Knowledge and Science. The right section showed women dancing and playing music. The left section showed three women chasing after an angel-like figure. This scene represented women seeking fame. Mary's painting honored the work of modern women.

After the fair, *Modern Woman* was removed from the Woman's Building. No one knows what happened to the painting after that. It was lost and probably destroyed. Only pictures remain of the painting.

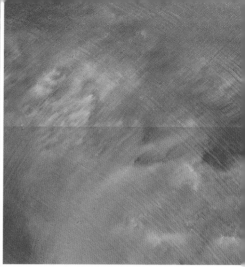

Edgar Degas bought *Girl Arranging Her Hair* from Mary. After his death, many people thought Degas had painted this painting. They did not think a woman could create such a skillful work of art.

Mary's Fame

In the early 1900s, Mary began to lose her sight. She could not see well enough to work during the last years of her life. On June 14, 1926, Mary died. She was 82.

Mary achieved a great deal as an artist. Her success gained respect for American artists. She introduced Americans to European styles of art. Mary also made people realize that women could be great artists.

In her art, Mary showed the importance of women. She hinted at women's intelligence by painting them reading and going to the theatre. Many of her paintings also showed women as caregivers.

Today, people can see Mary's art in museums. The Philadelphia Museum of Art in Pennsylvania and the Metropolitan Museum of Art in New York display many of her paintings and prints.

Important Dates

1844—Mary Cassatt is born May 22, in Allegheny City, Pennsylvania.

1851—Mary's family moves to Europe.

1860—Mary begins her studies at the Pennsylvania Academy of Fine Arts.

1861—The U.S. Civil War begins; the war ends in 1865.

1866—Mary moves to Paris, France, to study art.

1868—The Salon displays *The Mandolin Player*.

1871—The Great Fire of 1871 destroys much of downtown Chicago; many of Mary's early paintings are destroyed in the fire.

1877—Edgar Degas introduces Mary to the Impressionists.

1879—Mary exhibits her art with the Impressionists.

1880—Mary paints *Mother about to Wash Her Sleepy Child*.

1886—Mary paints *Girl Arranging Her Hair*.

1891—Mary shows her prints and paintings in a solo exhibit.

1893—*Modern Woman* is displayed in the Woman's Building at the World's Columbian Exposition in Chicago.

1914—World War I begins; the war ends in 1918.

1926—Mary dies June 14.

Words to Know

activist (AK-ti-vist)—a person who supports an important cause; during the late 1800s and early 1900s, many women activists fought for women's right to vote.

anatomy (uh-NAT-uh-mee)—the study of the human body

critic (KRIT-ik)—someone who reviews art, books, or movies

culture (KUHL-chur)—the way of life, ideas, customs, and traditions for a group of people

etching (ECH-ing)—a picture created on a metal plate; an artist uses an etching to make prints of a picture.

Impressionism (im-PREH-shuh-ni-zuhm)—an art style in which artists painted in broken brush strokes

mural (MYU-ruhl)—a large work of art on a wall or a ceiling

portrait (POR-trit)—a drawing or painting of a person

society (suh-SYE-uh-tee)—a large group of people who have similar interests, activities, and traditions

Read More

Giesecke, Ernestine. *Mary Cassatt.* The Life and Work Of. Des Plaines, Ill.: Heinemann, 2000.

Venezia, Mike. *Edgar Degas.* Getting to Know the World's Greatest Artists. New York: Children's Press, 2000.

Useful Addresses

National Gallery of Art
Mailing Address
2000B South Club Drive
Landover, MD 20785

Philadelphia Museum of Art
Benjamin Franklin Parkway
  and 26th Street
Philadelphia, PA 19130

Internet Sites

Do you want to find out more about Mary Cassatt? Let FactHound, our fact-finding hound dog, do the research for you.

Here's how:
1) Visit *http://www.facthound.com*.
2) Type in the **BOOK ID** number: **0736822291**.
3) Click on **FETCH IT**.

FactHound will fetch Internet sites picked by our editors just for you!

Index